Little Red Riding Hood

Adaptation and activities by Lisa Suett

Illustrated by Elena Prette

Young ELI Readers

Before you read

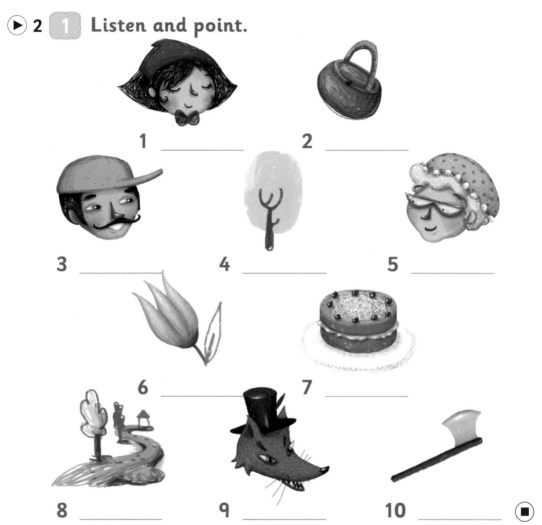

1 _____   2 _____

3 _____   4 _____   5 _____

6 _____   7 _____

8 _____   9 _____   10 _____ ■

2 Look and write the words below the
pictures in exercise 1.

path · the wolf · flower · Little Red Riding Hood tree · axe · basket · the woodcutter · cake · grandma

3 Help Little Red Riding Hood to find the path to grandma's house. Read the sentences and colour the houses.

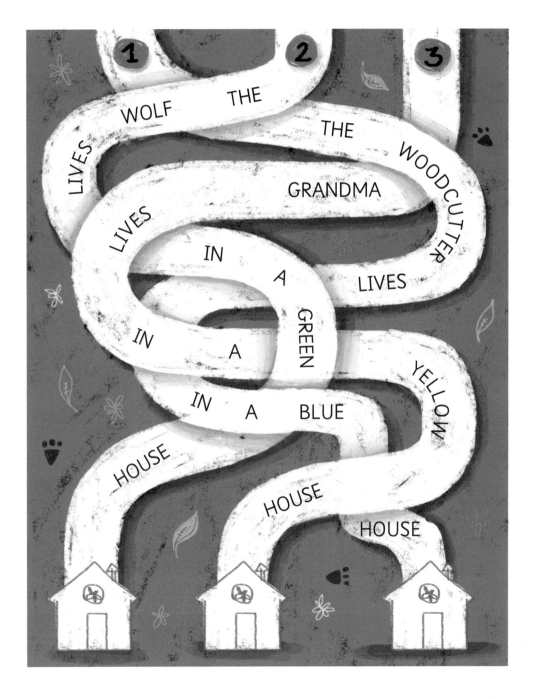

▶ 3 This is Little Red Riding Hood. She's got a red coat with a red hood. She lives with her mummy and daddy in a house in the woods. ■

▶ 4 *Red, red! I love red!*
I am Little Red Riding Hood.

Green like the grass
Blue like the sky
Yellow like the sun.

But red, red! I love red!
I am Little Red Riding Hood. ■

Colour the sun yellow.

1 Where does Little Red
Riding Hood live?_____

2 What colour is her coat?_____

3 Who does Little Red Riding Hood
live with?_____

5

5 One day mummy says, 'Grandma isn't well. Can you take this cake to grandma?'

What food can you see? Tick (✓).

☐ pears   ☐ biscuits   ☐ apples
☐ sandwiches   ☐ pizza   ☐ cake

What's your favourite food? _____

6

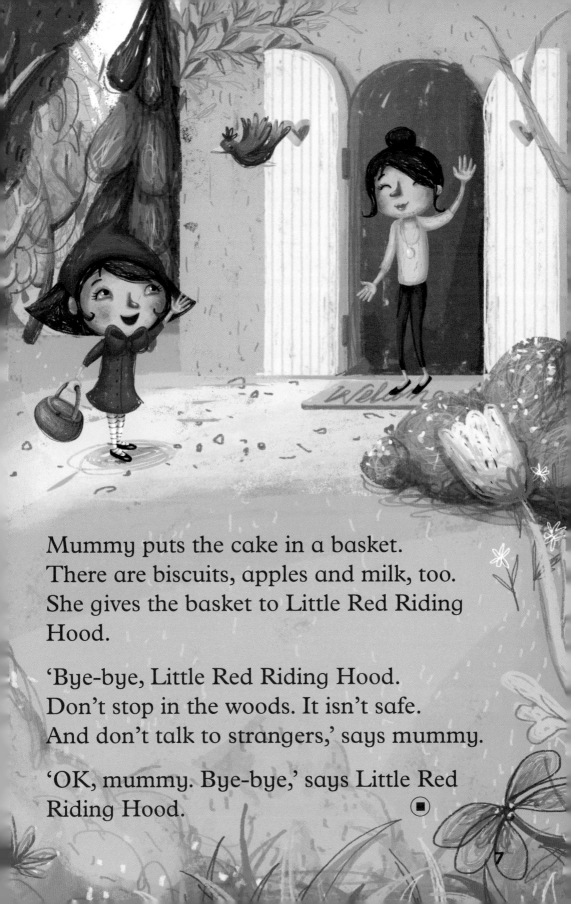

Mummy puts the cake in a basket.
There are biscuits, apples and milk, too.
She gives the basket to Little Red Riding
Hood.

'Bye-bye, Little Red Riding Hood.
Don't stop in the woods. It isn't safe.
And don't talk to strangers,' says mummy.

'OK, mummy. Bye-bye,' says Little Red
Riding Hood. ■

spider

▶ **6** Grandma's house is at the other end of the woods. Little Red Riding Hood walks on the path.

There are lots of animals in the woods.

squirrel

hedgehog

deer

ladybird

mouse

8

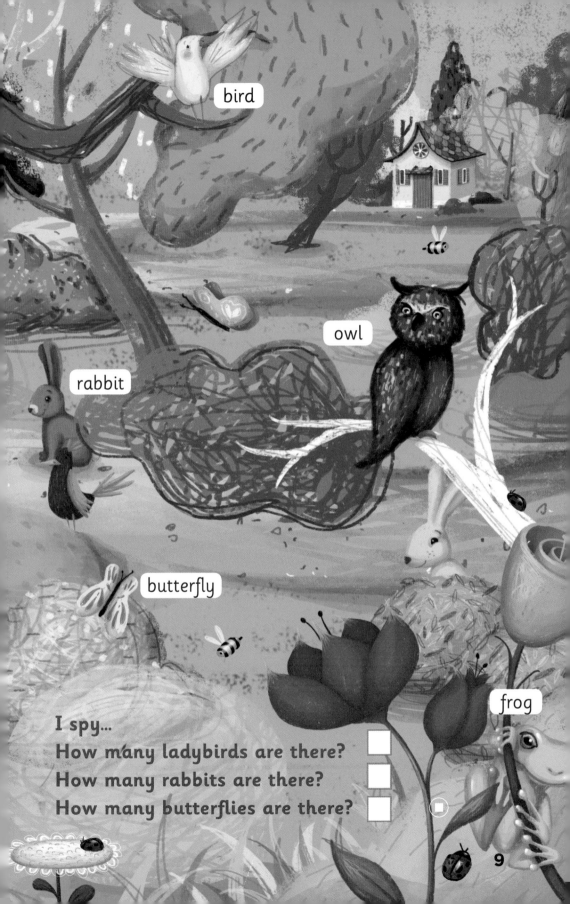

bird

owl

rabbit

butterfly

frog

I spy...
How many ladybirds are there? ☐
How many rabbits are there? ☐
How many butterflies are there? ☐

9

7 But in the woods there's a big bad wolf! He's got big eyes, big ears, a big nose and big teeth!

Little Red Riding Hood stops and picks
some flowers for grandma.
She picks blue and pink flowers. ▪

Colour the flowers in the basket.

▶ 8 *Look at the flowers*
red, pink and yellow
orange, white and blue.
Beautiful flowers all for you.
Grandma, grandma, here I come
Skip, skip, jump, jump, run, run, run! ▪

9 The big bad wolf sees Little Red Riding Hood.
'Where are you going, little girl?' he asks.
'I'm going to grandma's house. Grandma lives in
that yellow house,' says Little Red Riding Hood.
'And what have you got in the basket?'
asks the wolf.
'I've got a cake, biscuits, apples and milk for
grandma,' says Little Red Riding Hood.

12

What's in the basket?

LMIK ▢▢▢▢

PLEPAS ▢▢▢▢▢▢

KCAE ▢▢▢▢

SCIBUSTI ▢▢▢▢▢▢▢▢

13

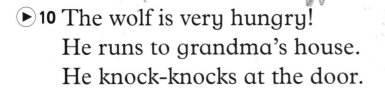

10 The wolf is very hungry!
He runs to grandma's house.
He knock-knocks at the door.

'Who is it?' asks grandma.
'Hello, grandma. It's Little Red Riding
Hood,' says the wolf.
'Come in, my dear!' says grandma.

The wolf goes in and eats poor grandma!

Little Red Riding Hood is at grandma's house. She knock-knocks and says, 'Hello, grandma. It's me, Little Red Riding Hood.' 'Come in, my dear!' says the wolf. Little Red Riding Hood thinks it's grandma. ▣

11 Little Red Riding Hood goes into the bedroom. She looks at grandma.

'Oh grandma!
You've got big ⬜⬜⬜⬜ .'
'I've got big eyes to see you.'
'And grandma,
you've got big ⬜⬜⬜⬜ .'
'Yes, I've got big ears to hear you.'
'And grandma,
you've got a big ⬜⬜⬜⬜ .'
'Yes, I've got a big nose to smell you.'
'But grandma,
you've got big ⬜⬜⬜⬜⬜ .'
'Yes, I've got BIG teeth to eat YOU!'

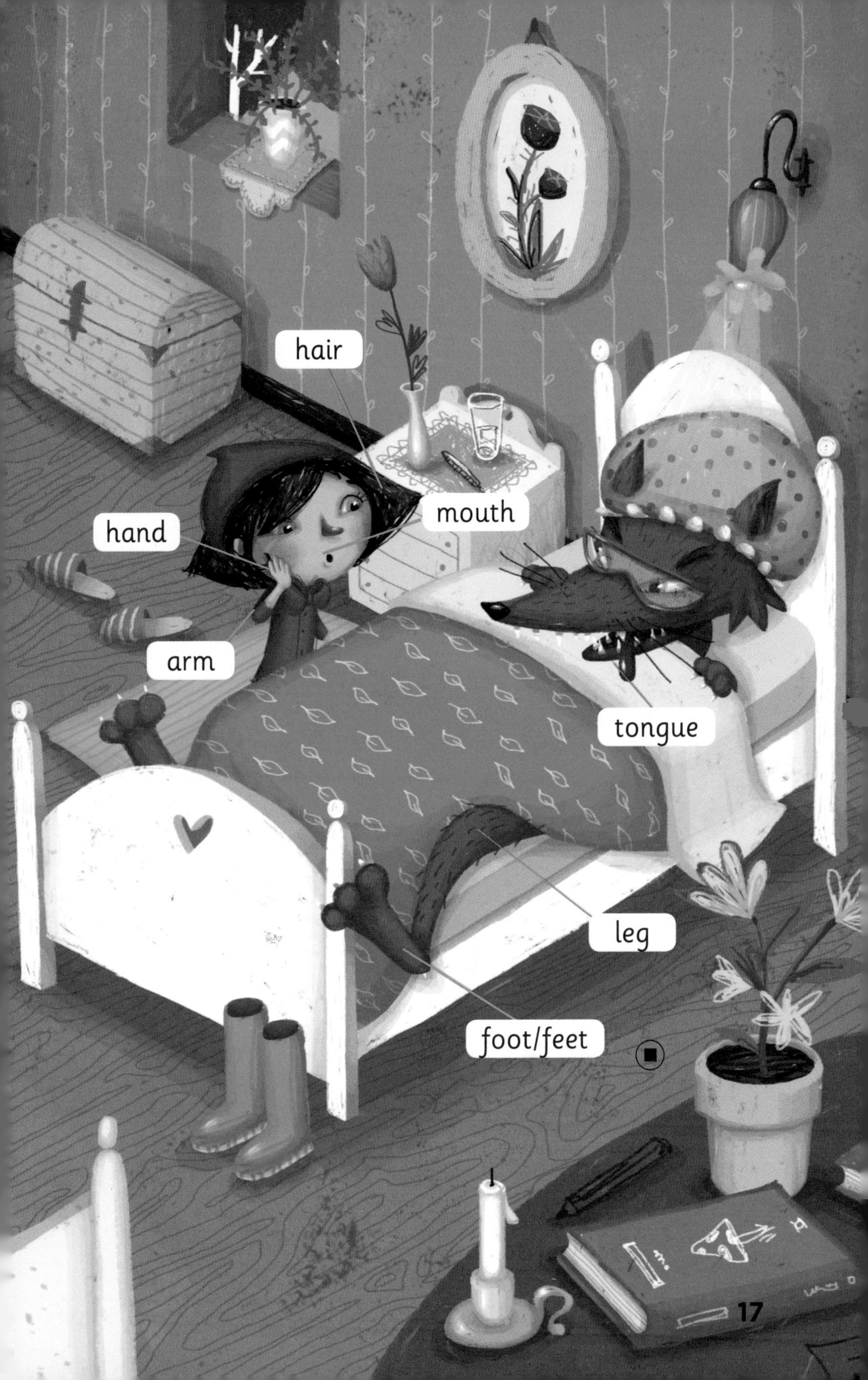

hair

hand

mouth

arm

tongue

leg

foot/feet

12 'Help! It's the big bad wolf!' says Little Red Riding Hood.

Look at the pictures and match them to the verbs.

| run · jump · dance · skip |

1 _____ 2 _____ 3 _____ 4 _____

A woodcutter is in the woods. He hears Little Red Riding Hood and runs to grandma's house.

'It's the big bad wolf!' says the woodcutter.

He takes an axe and cuts open the wolf. Grandma jumps out! Grandma and Little Red Riding Hood are safe now. ■

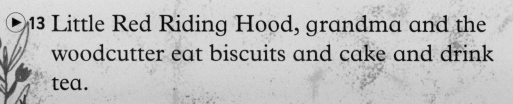

▶**13** Little Red Riding Hood, grandma and the woodcutter eat biscuits and cake and drink tea.

'I'm sorry, grandma. Mummy is right. It isn't safe to stop in the woods,' says Little Red Riding Hood. ■

Use the secret code to find the message from Little Red Riding Hood.

| A ♥ | E 👄 | G ♡ | N ☀ | R 🍦 | S 🌀 | T ☆ |

Always be careful!
Don't talk to __ __ __ __ __ __ __ __ __

🌀 ☆ 🍦 ♥ ☀ ♡ 👄 🍦 🌀

Puppets

You need:
- a toilet roll
- a pencil
- paper
- scissors
- glue
- paints and a paintbrush

1

Take a toilet roll.

2

Fold the top to make the ears.

3

Draw a face on a piece of paper.

4

Cut out and stick.

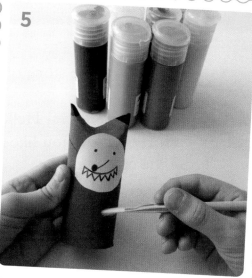

5

Paint your puppet.

6

Play with your puppets.

You can make puppets of the wolf, Little Red Riding Hood, grandma and the woodcutter. Use your puppets to tell the story.

Let's act!

NARRATOR This is the story of Little Red Riding Hood.

LRRH [*arrives and waves*] Hello! My name's Little Red Riding Hood. Do you like my red coat and red hood? I love the colour red.

CAST [*all sing together*] Red, red! I love red!
I am Little Red Riding Hood.
Green like the grass
Blue like the sky
Yellow like the sun.
But red, red! I love red!
I am Little Red Riding Hood.

NARRATOR One day mummy calls Little Red Riding Hood.

MUMMY Little Red Riding Hood!
LRRH [*enters on stage*] Yes, mummy.
MUMMY Grandma isn't well. Take her this cake.
NARRATOR Mummy gives Little Red Riding Hood a basket.
MUMMY [*putting the food in the basket*] There is a cake. There are biscuits. There are apples. There is some milk. Oh, and remember. Don't stop in the woods. Don't talk to strangers!

LRRH OK, mummy. Bye-bye!
MUMMY Bye-bye!

NARRATOR Little Red Riding Hood walks on the path. She is happy but she doesn't see the big bad wolf.

THE WOLF [*behind a tree*] Mmmm, I'm hungry.

LRRH [*stops to pick flowers*] Look at the beautiful flowers. Grandma likes flowers.

CAST [*all sing together*] *Look at the flowers*
red, pink and yellow
orange, white and blue.
Beautiful flowers all for you.
Grandma, grandma, here I come
Skip, skip, jump, jump, run, run, run!

THE WOLF Hello, little girl. What's your name?
LRRH Hello. I'm Little Red Riding Hood.
THE WOLF Where are you going?
LRRH I'm going to grandma's house.
THE WOLF And what have you got in the basket?
LRRH I've got a cake, biscuits, apples and milk for grandma.
THE WOLF Where does grandma live?
LRRH [*points*] Grandma lives in that yellow house.
THE WOLF [*waves bye-bye*] Bye-bye, Little Red Riding Hood.
LRRH Bye-bye.
NARRATOR The wolf is very hungry!

THE WOLF [*knocking at the door*] Knock knock!
GRANDMA Who is it?

THE WOLF It's me. It's Little Red Riding Hood.
GRANDMA Come in!

NARRATOR The wolf goes in and eats poor grandma.
Later, Little Red Riding Hood arrives.

LRRH [*knocking at the door*] Grandma, it's me!
THE WOLF Come in, my dear.
LRRH Grandma, you've got big eyes.
THE WOLF Yes, I've got big eyes to see you.
LRRH Grandma, you've got big ears.
THE WOLF Yes, I've got big ears to hear you.
LRRH Grandma, you've got a big nose.
THE WOLF Yes, I've got a big nose to smell you.
LRRH Grandma, you've got big teeth.
THE WOLF Yes, I've got big teeth to eat you!
[*The wolf jumps out of bed and runs after Little Red Riding Hood.*]
LRRH HELP!!!

NARRATOR Outside a woodcutter hears Little Red Riding Hood.

[*The woodcutter runs to grandma's house.*]
THE WOODCUTTER It's alright, Little Red Riding Hood.
I've got my axe. I can help grandma.

NARRATOR The woodcutter has got an axe. He cuts open the wolf. Grandma jumps out!

THE WOODCUTTER Now you're safe.
LRRH + GRANDMA Thank you!

First **ELi** Readers

Jane Cadwallader

MARTHA AND THE TIGER PARTY

Illustrated by Gustavo Mazali

[*The woodcutter, grandma and Little Red Riding Hood sit in the kitchen and have tea and cake.*]

LRRH Mummy is right. It isn't safe to stop in the woods. And don't talk to strangers!

THE END

Activities – Play time

1 Find and circle the words that rhyme.

1 red	basket	bed	cake
2 tea	door	floor	hood
3 stop	flower	knock	wolf

2 Find the words and match them to the pictures.

3 Look at pages 8-9. Circle the correct answer.

1 How many birds are there? *Three | Six*
2 How many frogs are there? *Two | Five*
3 How many flowers are there? *Four | Eight*
4 How many rabbits are there? *Three | One*

4 Find 7 animal words. Then use the other letters to make the sentence.

L	A	D	Y	B	I	R	D
S	Q	U	I	R	R	E	L
G	R	A	N	D	M	M	A
H	E	D	G	E	H	O	G
L	I	E	O	K	E	U	S
S	T	E	W	R	A	S	W
B	E	R	L	R	R	E	Y
B	I	R	D	C	A	K	E

_ _ _ _ _ _ _   _ _ _ _ _

_ _ _ _ _ _ _ _ _ _   _ _ _ _.

5 Circle the correct words.
Then complete the sentences.

1 Grandma lives in a _____ house.

  yellow   green   pink

2 Take grandma this _____ .

  book   pizza   cake

3 Don't stop in the _____ .

  supermarket   park   woods

4 Little Red Riding Hood talks to a

_____ .

  rabbit   wolf   boy

6 True or false? Tick (✓).

	T	F
1 Little Red Riding Hood has got biscuits in the basket.	☐	☐
2 Little Red Riding Hood stops to pick fruit.	☐	☐
3 The wolf is thirsty.	☐	☐
4 The wolf eats grandma.	☐	☐
5 Little Red Riding Hood has got big eyes and big teeth.	☐	☐
6 The woodcutter helps mummy.	☐	☐

7 There's a new animal in the woods.
Read and draw the animal.

It's got big eyes.
It's got a small
nose.
It eats flowers.
It's got two little
hands.
It's got a big
mouth and big
teeth.
It's got black hair.
It's got two big feet
and a blue tongue.

8 Complete the song.

| jump · red · you · run · flowers · skip · white |

Look at the __ __ __ __ __ __ __
__ __ __, pink and yellow
orange, __ __ __ __ __ __ and blue.
Beautiful flowers all for __ __ __
Grandma, grandma, here I come
__ __ __ __ __, skip, __ __ __ __ __, jump,
__ __ __ __, run, run!

9 Play the game. You need a dice and a counter.

10 Put the story in the correct order.

a ○ b ○ c ○

d ○ e ○ f ○

MARTHA AND HER FRIENDS
ARE READING.

▶ 3 TESSA WANTS TO GO
TO TAMMY'S BIRTHDAY PARTY.

A PARTY!
TODAY!
HURRAH!

4

4 TESSA'S FRIENDS HELP.
SID WASHES TESSA'S EARS.

6

5 BERTIE WASHES TESSA'S FEET.

CHAPTER 2: LET'S GO TO THE PARTY!

BUT... HERE
COMES SANCHO.

NOW TESSA'S READY.
AND SANCHO'S GOT A PRESENT.

8 EVERYONE GOES TO THE PARTY.
SANCHO'S GOT THE PRESENT.

*WE'RE OFF TO THE
PARTY. COME ALONG!
COME ALONG!*

OH, NO! SANCHO
IS FALLING!

BE
CAREFUL,
SANCHO!

10 TESSA HELPS SANCHO.

19

CHAPTER 4:
TESSA IS A WONDERFUL TIGER!

13 EVERYONE GOES TO THE PARTY.
SANCHO'S GOT THE PRESENT.

WE'RE OFF TO THE
PARTY. COME ALONG!
COME ALONG!

ACTIVITY PAGES

1 COLOUR THE FRAMES OF THE PICTURES THAT ARE IN THE STORY.

2 COLOUR THE PRESENT THEY TAKE TO THE PARTY.

3 DRAW ARROWS TO SHOW THE ORDER OF THE STORY.

4 COLOUR TESSA AND TAMMY.

FINISH COLOURING THE ANIMALS. MATCH
THEM WITH WHAT THEY USE TO CLEAN TESSA.

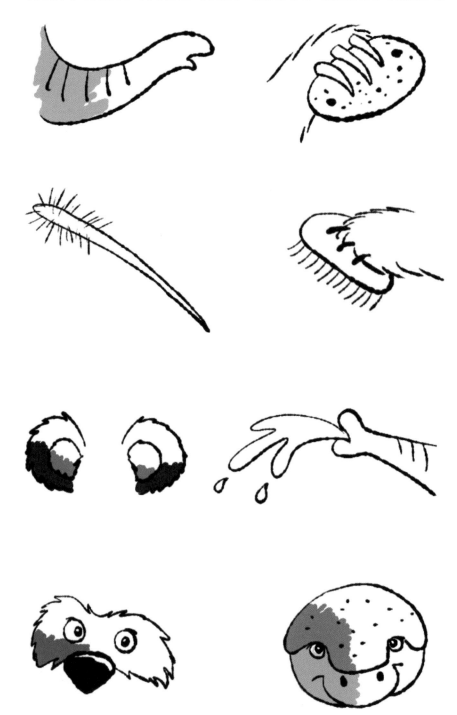

6 COLOUR THE TAILS OF THE SQUIRRELS THAT ARE DOING THE SAME ACTION.

7 DECORATE TAMMY'S BIRTHDAY CAKE.

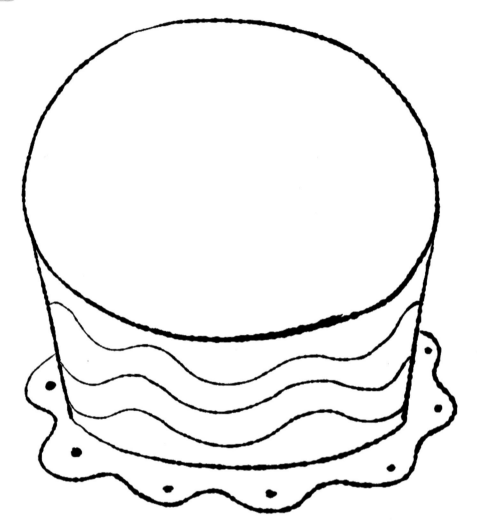

8 DO YOU LIKE THE STORY? DRAW YOUR FACE.

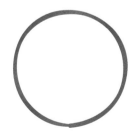 = I LOVE THE STORY!

 = I LIKE THE STORY.

= I QUITE LIKE THE STORY.

 = I DON'T LIKE THE STORY.